CW01211688

Believe in me

Living with a learning disability

Written by Natalie Duo and Honor Head
Illustrated by Sue Downing

In aid of mencap

FRANKLIN WATTS
LONDON • SYDNEY

First published in Great Britain in 2024 by Franklin Watts

© Hodder and Stoughton, 2024. All rights reserved

Managing editor: Victoria Brooker / Design: Gemma Steward
ISBN: 9781445187358 (hbk) / ISBN: 9781445187341 (pbk)

Some of the definitions in this book have been provided by Mencap.

Franklin Watts, an imprint of Hachette Children's Group
Part of Hodder and Stoughton
Carmelite House, 50 Victoria Embankment, London EC4Y 0DZ

An Hachette UK Company

www.hachette.co.uk
www.hachettechildrens.co.uk

Printed and bound in China

MIX
Paper | Supporting responsible forestry
FSC® C104740

Contents

Foreword	4
I am Natalie Duo	6
What is a learning disability?	8
Disability or difficulty?	10
Help and support	12
Why does it happen?	14
What's it like having a learning disability?	16
Talk to me!	18
Be friendly	20
Be positive	22
Share the dream	24
My family	26
Don't ignore me!	28
Little things count	30
School life	32
Staying safe online	34
The right to work	36
Your life, your way!	38
Last word from Natalie	40
Glossary	42
Notes for parents and carers	44
About Mencap	46
Websites	47
Index	48

Foreword

My name is Natalie Duo and I have a learning disability. I wrote this book because I want to help young people without a learning disability understand what it's like to have a learning disability. I want everyone to see that having a learning disability is something to be proud of. I really hope you will enjoy reading my book as much as I have enjoyed writing it.

Natalie Duo

5

I am Natalie Duo

My name is Natalie Duo and I have a learning disability. When I was diagnosed with a learning disability, it was hard for my mum to get me the right help.

Because I found out quite late, I was already a long way behind the other children in my class. I did not learn to read until I was fourteen, but that has not stopped me getting a brilliant job that I love.

I work for Mencap as a Co-Trainer. Mencap is a charity that supports people of all ages who have a learning disability. I work on Learning Disability Awareness sessions for employers and act as an ambassador.

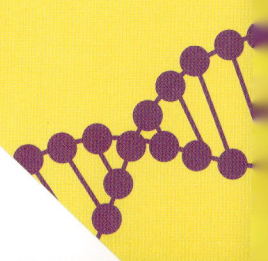

As an ambassador, I go to company conferences and talk to people about my experiences as someone who has a learning disability. I talk about what it means to have a learning disability and how they can employ people like me and help us to have successful careers.

I have run information sessions at the NHS and the Houses of Parliament. I have also been on TV and the radio to speak about learning disabilities and employment. I always wanted to be a writer and now I have written this book to help others.

What is a learning disability?

A learning disability is to do with the way a person's brain works. Having a learning disability makes it harder for someone to learn, understand or do things.

There are different types of learning disability, which can be mild, moderate, severe or profound. Having a learning disability affects each person in a different way.

People with a learning disability tend to take longer to learn and may need support to develop new skills, understand complicated information and interact with other people.

Natalie says ...

I hope this book will inspire children with learning disabilities to believe in themselves and what they can achieve. I also want children without learning disabilities to know what it is like to have one, so they understand us and help to support us.

People with a severe learning disability or profound and multiple learning disability (PMLD), will need more care and support with areas such as mobility, personal care and communication. People with a moderate learning disability may also need support in these areas, but not definitely.

People with a learning disability may take longer to learn new things, not just at school but when they are older, too. They may need more time to understand complicated information or instructions.

Whatever challenges people face, families, friends and schoolmates can make it easier by being kind and helpful.

Disability or difficulty?

A learning disability is not the same as a learning difficulty. They are very different.

Dyslexia is a type of learning difficulty as it is a barrier to learning. Unlike a learning disability, a learning difficulty does not impact on the person's intellect. People with a learning difficulty can also have a learning disability.

Someone with a learning difficulty, such as dyslexia, might get their words muddled, so they might read 'pat' instead of 'tap'. Someone with a learning disability might not be able to read the word at all.

People with a learning disability are often affected physically in many different ways. Some may have trouble moving about or doing simple tasks.

It can be very easy to try and do everything for someone with a learning disability, but we should try and support people with a learning disability to do as much for themselves as possible.

Help and support

The level of support someone needs depends on the person. Some people with profound disabilities may need a lot of support.

They may need to go to a school where they have special teachers, resources and equipment that will help them be able to learn.

Some children go to a local primary school and then move on to a special secondary school where they can get extra support.

As adults, people with a learning disability may live in their own home but with support from carers so that they can live more independently. This means people with a learning disability can live by themselves, but there is someone to help, if needed, with certain tasks. A person with more serious learning disabilities might need care and support all the time. Other people with a learning disability will need only very small amounts of support.

Why does it happen?

A learning disability happens when the brain is still developing, before, during or soon after the mother gives birth.

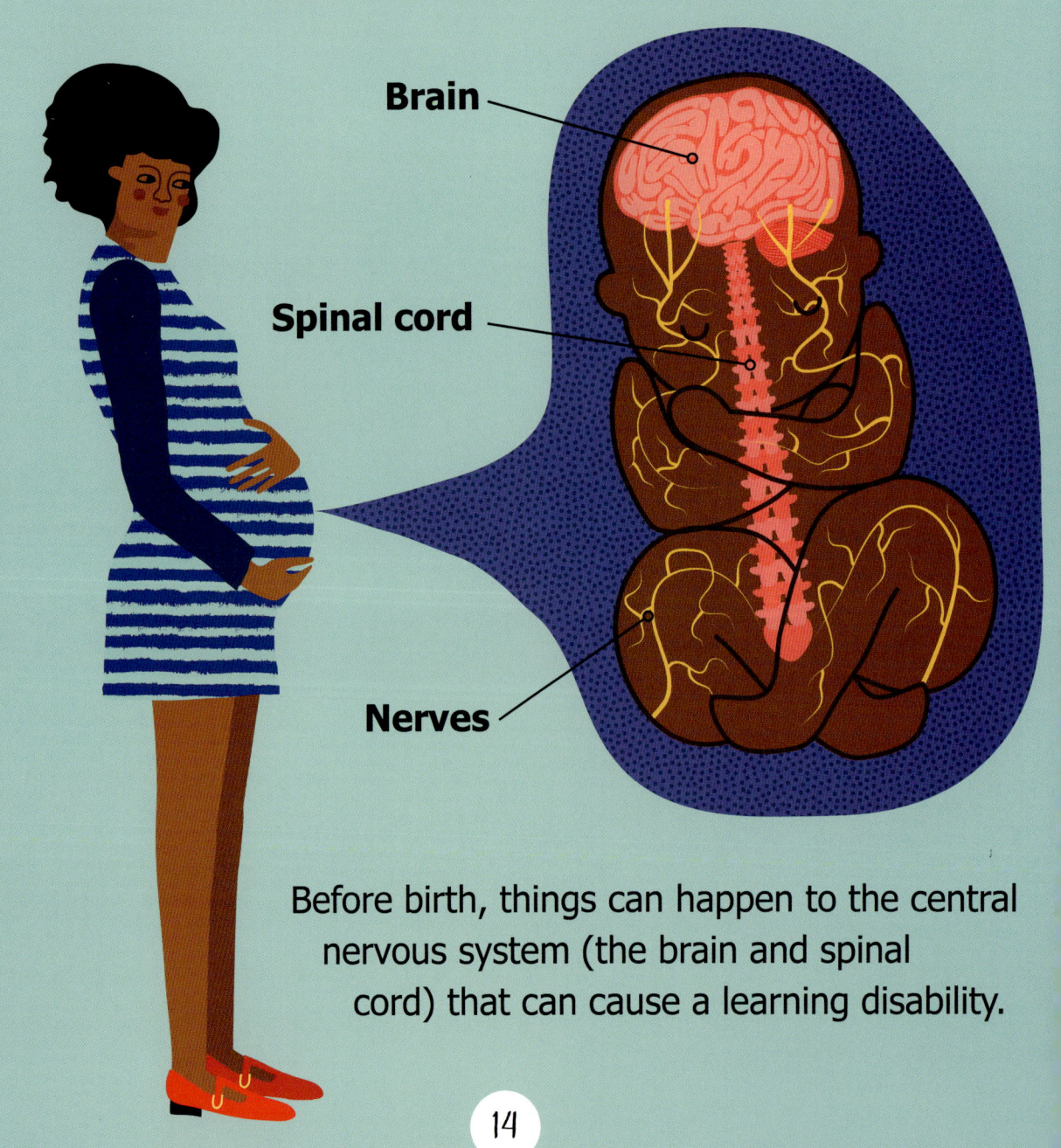

Brain

Spinal cord

Nerves

Before birth, things can happen to the central nervous system (the brain and spinal cord) that can cause a learning disability.

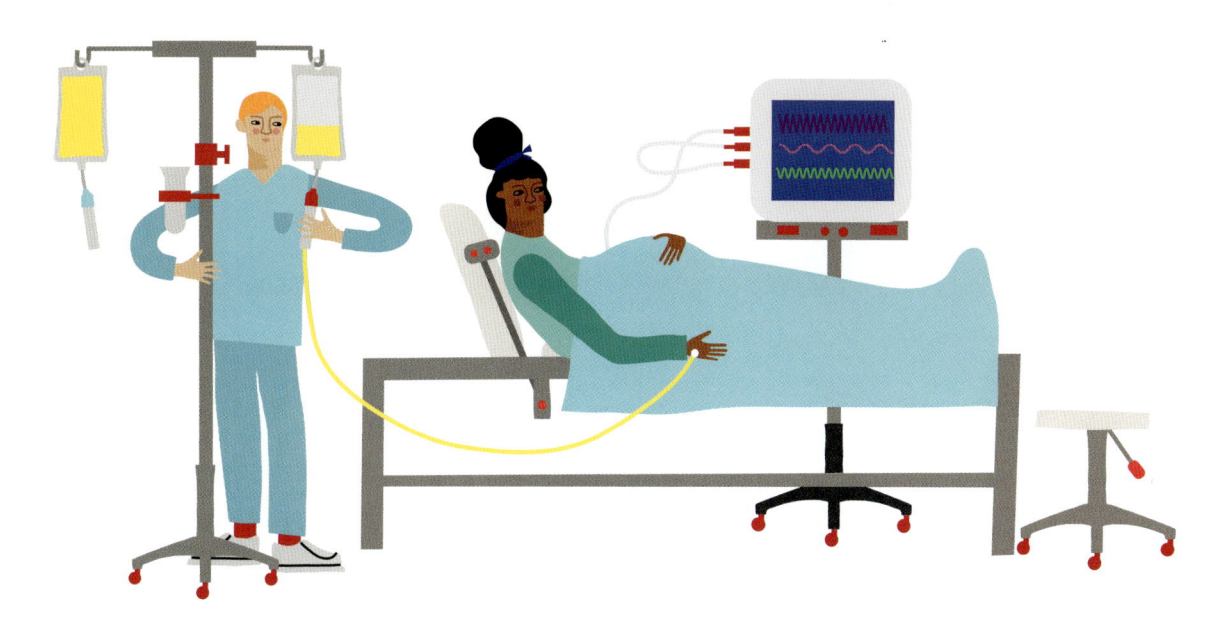

A child can be born with a learning disability if the mother has an accident or is ill while she is pregnant. It can happen at birth if a baby does not get enough oxygen during childbirth or is born too early.

A child can have a learning disability if they have certain genes. Genes contain information about you, such as the colour of your hair and eyes. They are passed on to you from your parents. Genes are inside cells in your body.

After birth, a learning disability can be caused by childhood illnesses or accidents. These things don't happen very often.

What's it like having a learning disability?

People with a learning disability usually learn at a different pace from everyone else and there are lots of ways they can learn.

Some people may not speak. This can be known as being non-verbal, and they can use different forms of communication like Makaton, which is a language programme that combines signs, symbols and speech to give different options for people to communicate. Using signs can help people who do not use speech.

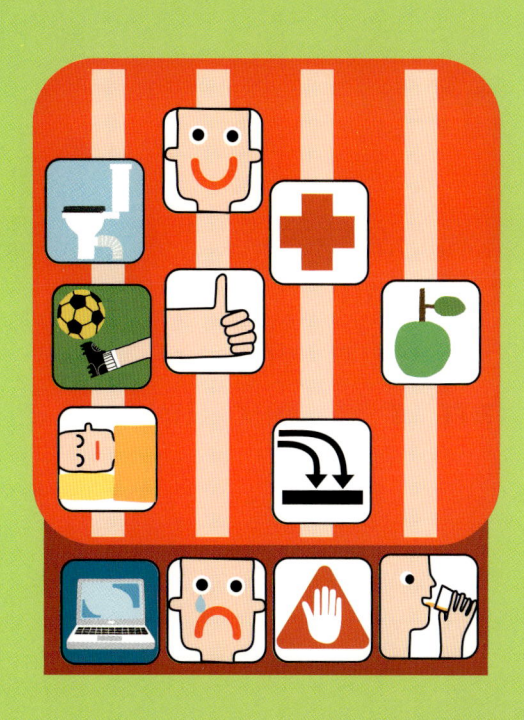

PECS, which stands for Picture Exchange Communication System, is a type of additional and alternative communication that uses visual symbols. This can be useful for people who have difficulty with speaking or verbal communication.

Natalie says ...

When I was younger I felt very sad. I would cry a lot because I couldn't understand why I was different from everyone else. When I went to primary school, I just wanted to be accepted as myself, as a person like everyone else. I felt much better when I went to my secondary school, which was a school for people with learning disabilities. For the first time I didn't stand out.

Talk to me!

Learning to communicate with family, friends and the outside world is hard work for everyone, but it is even harder for people with a learning disability.

When you are talking to a person with a learning disability, it is helpful if you can try to do the following:

Listen

- Be patient if the person speaks slowly.
- Remember that not every person with a learning disability is verbal – some people use Makaton, which uses signs and symbols to help people communicate.

Learn

- Don't speak too fast.
- Use simple words and speak clearly.

Natalie says ...

I had a stutter because of my learning disability. This made me compare myself to others in a bad way. I was able to overcome this in my teens when I accepted that I was always going to stutter. I became more confident and comfortable with my stutter. Now, if I feel like I'm going to stutter, I speak slowly to avoid it so that I get my point across and make sure I am listened to.

Ask

- If the person is taking longer than usual to reply, ask if they are okay.

- Make sure the person has understood what you said.

- Ask questions. People with a learning disability are often happy to share information about themselves.

- Most people with a learning disability can talk about all sorts of things, just like anyone else.

Be friendly

When you meet anyone for the first time, you smile and are friendly. It is just the same when you first meet someone with a learning disability.

When you want to talk to someone with a learning disability be friendly and smile. Don't stare, just be natural. Most people are a bit nervous when meeting new people and people with a learning disability can be extra anxious when making friends. Be patient and calm.

There are a few things to remember when getting to know a person with a learning disability.

• Talking face-to-face is best for most people with a learning disability.

• Don't be afraid to ask the person to repeat something they've said if you didn't understand it the first time.

Be positive

Having a learning disability can affect people's self-esteem and self-confidence. Staying positive can help.

Self-esteem is how you see yourself and what you think of yourself. People with a learning disability might think they are not as good as other people. They might not be able to do things in the same way as people without a learning disability, such as playing sports. But everyone is different and has their own strengths.

It is important to be positive with people who have a learning disability. Don't tease them or be unkind about things they can't do, but be positive and encouraging about the things they can do. Having a learning disability doesn't mean a person can't do something. They might just do it in a different way.

Help to build someone's self-confidence by being supportive and helping them with the things they can do to improve that skill. Do a high-five and give praise if something goes well. Everyone needs practice and time to improve their skills.

Share the dream

Having a learning disability might mean a person struggles more to achieve something, but they can still set goals like anyone else.

Like everyone, people with a learning disability have hopes and dreams and plans for the future. The dream could be to do something most of us take for granted, such as going to the cinema. Or it could be a big dream for the future, like being a scientist. With support from those around them, they can find the best way to achieve their goals and dreams.

At school and at home, talk about ways you can help someone you know with a learning disability achieve their goal. This could be by doing something practical to help, discussing a different way of doing something or just by giving encouragement.

Natalie says ...

We often see more positives in life than someone without a learning disability. Because it can take more effort to achieve something, we celebrate our achievements more.

My family

Positive family support is very important to help children with a learning disability thrive and have the best start in life.

For many people, their families often understand best how a person's learning disability affects them each day and what support they need.

Many families have to spend time getting the right support for their loved ones, such as adaptions at school, medical help or care at home. Without this support, this person might find daily life difficult.

Families of a person with a learning disability can sometimes be referred to as family carers. A carer is somebody who looks after a family member who needs help to properly care for themselves. You may have friends who are carers for their siblings. Being a family carer or young carer can sometimes be challenging.

Natalie says ...

In my family I was the only person to have a learning disability. The most important thing I wanted my family, especially my siblings, to do was to see me for who I am and not just my learning disability.

There are lots of places people who are a carer can get support (see page 47).

Don't ignore me!

No one wants to feel left out of making plans or planning activities.

People with a learning disability have their own opinions, likes and dislikes. Don't ignore them. Ask them what they think.

Most people with a learning disability will want to have a go like anyone else. Always look at how to adapt activities if needed, rather than assuming someone can't be involved. Try to avoid activities where they are left out and have to watch other people doing it, unless they are happy to watch. Whether it's a visit to a museum, cinema or trampolining, there are lots of ways to include everyone.

For example, you might want to watch a video of a similar activity before you visit to make the person you are going with aware of what to expect. You could read a story or look at photographs of different places to decide what you would like to do together.

If it's an activity you have done before, you can describe it to the person you will be going with to give them an idea of what to expect.

Little things count

There are many ways you can support someone in your family, or who is close to you, if they have a learning disability.

Every person with a learning disability is different, so it's very important that you don't assume they can't do something. Let them know you can help if they need it but remember many people with a learning disability are independent and do lots of everyday tasks for themselves.

Natalie says...

A great way my sister supported me growing up was when we were watching TV. If a complicated word came up that I didn't understand, my sister would find a simpler word to use so I could understand.

Also, I struggle with cutting meat so when I'm at family events and people are cooking food for me, they will always cut up the food before they give it to me so it's easier for me to eat.

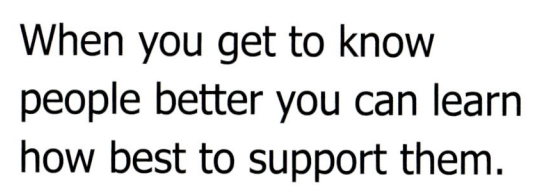

When you get to know people better you can learn how best to support them.

School life

School can be hard sometimes for children with a learning disability. But there are lots of ways their classmates can help to support them.

Always be respectful and friendly to anyone you are talking to. Ask about their hobbies, pets and favourite things. You may discover that you have a lot in common.

Natalie says...

At school I felt like I wasn't treated the same as people that didn't have a learning disability. I feel like I missed out on a lot of things that people without a learning disability were able to experience. For example, I knew that the majority of people at school were able to go to prom, but I never had the opportunity to go to one. This made me feel disappointed, sad and left out.

Some people with a learning disability may speak in a different way or not at all. Be patient and calm when talking to them. Wait for them to give you a response in a conversation. Sometimes they might need a little time to think about what they want to say. Listen carefully to what they say.

Make sure you include people with a learning disability in social events in and out of school. Some children with learning disabilities really miss out on the experience of going out with school friends.

Staying safe online

Being online is important and it is a part of everyday life. Like everyone else, those with learning disabilities have to take care and stay safe online too.

The internet is a great place for people with learning disabilities as it can be a way to learn, stay in touch and feel part of the community. People with a learning disability sometimes find it easier to communicate with others online rather than face-to-face.

Being able to take their time to write an email or text can be easier than having to think of something to say quickly on the spot. And they can read online messages as many times as they need to help them process what is being said. But being online can lead to cyberbullying. If you are part of an online group and anyone is being bullied, don't join in. Make sure you report it to an adult, such as a parent, carer or teacher, who can help.

At school, offer to help those with a learning disability if they are trying to find a safe site or suggest a teacher or school librarian who can help them.

The right to work

Everyone has the right to work and earn money. The more support people with a learning disability get, the more they will be able to enjoy working life.

Today, people with a learning disability have a wide range of jobs and careers. From working behind the scenes in cinemas and theatres, to acting or dancing on stage. Or working in the car or aerospace industries. People with a learning disability should be given the same opportunities to work as everyone else.

Charities such as Mencap work with employers to help them realise that people with a learning disability can be valuable members of their workforce. They partner with companies to offer opportunities to learn new skills and move into paid roles.

37

Your life, your way!

With the right support, everyone with a learning disability has the opportunity to live their life the way they want to.

Most people with a learning disability can achieve their dreams, they may just have to do it with a bit more support and in a different way.

We all need some form of support as we go through life, for example training when you start a new job. When a person has a learning disability, they might face extra challenges when they are grown up, for example, understanding everyday things, such as using money. There are many organisations that can give support to people at these times, such as Mencap, but family and friends can help, too. With the right support, people with a learning disability can achieve great things.

Good job, team!

Last word from Natalie

Everyone deserves to be treated with respect and this goes for people with learning disabilities and difficulties as well as everyone else.

I was only nineteen years old when I started working at Mencap and I was quite shy. But when I held my first information session, I discovered I loved presenting and making people laugh!

If you talk about what you want to do when you leave school, remember that people with a learning disability also have their own dreams about the future. Most people with a learning disability can achieve their dreams if they have the right support.

In the future I would like to continue to write more books as well as continuing to work for Mencap. I want to reach more companies, big and small, to encourage them to employ people with learning disabilities by making them realise how much people with a learning disability have to offer.

We all need some form of help as we go through life, for example training when you start a new job. When a person has a learning disability, they might face extra challenges when they are grown up.

There are many organisations, such as Mencap, that can give support to people at these times, but family and friends can help, too. With the right support, people with a learning disability can achieve great things.

With the right support, everyone can achieve their goals!

Glossary

adaption – changing something to make it work in a different way

ambassador – someone who speaks on behalf of someone else or on behalf of an organisation such as Mencap

careers – a job that someone chooses to do

communication – sharing messages or information

cyberbullying – bullying that happens online

dyslexia – a learning disorder that means it's difficult for some people to recognise and understand written words

Houses of Parliament – where the UK government hold meetings

instructions – information about how to do something

mobility – being able to move about from place to place

NHS – the National Health Service is an organisation in the UK that helps people to get better when they are ill

online – being connected to or using the internet

personal care – looking after yourself by doing things such as brushing your hair, or cleaning your teeth

prom – a party for children in their last year of school

stutter – a speech difficulty where someone finds it hard to say some words without repeating them or saying part of the word. Also known as a stammer.

support – help

Notes for parents and carers

If you think your child may have a learning disability, speak to a doctor (GP) or your health visitor for advice. Getting the support of your health visitor and GP is often the first step. If your child has not received a diagnosis but you have concerns about their development you should contact your GP, who should be able to offer advice and refer you to a specialist if necessary.

Whether you are waiting for a diagnosis or not, there are some things you can do to help your child.

The best thing you can do is to help your child help themselves. This means building up their confidence, self-esteem and resilience. There is no denying that they will face challenges throughout life, but attitudes are changing and with the right support, encouragement and life skills they should be able to grow and thrive.

It will sometimes be hard but always try to stay strong and positive for your child. Seek out any help you can get and if you are concerned about any aspect of your child's support, you have the right to bring this up with the people involved, and to challenge the decisions being made for you and your child so you both get the support you need. Getting the right support when your child is young can transform their future.

Be your own expert. Learn as much as you can about your child's disability and any education programmes or other forms of help they are entitled to. Contact your local authority for details on how to get an Education, Health and Care Plan. This can be a long and difficult process but is well worth it to give your child the support they deserve.

Try to maintain a sense of perspective and a sense of humour – and that won't always be easy! As they grow your child will take their lead from you. If you stay focused and optimistic your child is more likely to do the same.

There will be bad days. Allow your child to be angry, resentful, frustrated and sad. Help them to cope with these emotions. Be there for them – sometimes just being held or having a hug is all that is needed.

Be aware of anxiety and stress – some children may want to hide it from you. Be aware of how they are sleeping, if they become withdrawn, closed down, agitated or are displaying challenging behaviours like hitting. Talk to your child about how they feel. Practise mindfulness and breathing exercises to help with stress. Seek expert help if you need to.

Don't keep your child away from other family members. Make sure the child is included in all family activities. If you have other children, make sure they don't feel left out or feel all your time is being given to one child. Let them help where possible.

About mencap

There are many organisations and charities that help parents and carers of children with learning disabilities. They can help with general advice and guidance and practical matters such as education choices and benefits. Mencap is one of the biggest in the UK.

Mencap was established in 1946 to promote valuing and supporting people with a learning disability, their families and carers. The Mencap vision is a world where people with a learning disability are valued equally, listened to and included.

Mencap promotes the rights of those with a learning disability to be treated with respect and kindness and to be considered as valuable members of society. Mencap do a lot of campaigning and policy work to achieve this, as well as supporting people into work and providing supported housing and care services.

A big part of this is to help companies and organisations to train and employ people with a learning disability so that they can earn a wage and support themselves.

Websites

Mencap.org.uk
Mencap is a national charity that supports people with learning disabilities and their parents and carers. Explore the website for a whole range of information:
www.mencap.org.uk

HelpGuide.org
HelpGuide run a mental health information website. For specific information on helping children with learning disabilities, see:
www.helpguide.org/articles/autism-learning-disabilities/helping-children-with-learning-disabilities.htm

Singinghands.co.uk
Singing Hands run workshops and sessions for people of all ages and abilities to learn Makaton.

Carers.org
The Carers Trust are a support organisation for people who provide unpaid care support for family or friends.

Index

achievements 23, 24–25, 38–39
assumptions 28, 30
anxiety 20, 45

babies 14–15
birth 14–15
bullying 35
brain 8, 14

careers 6–7, 24, 36, 39, 40, 46
carers 13, 27, 46
causes of learning disabilities 14–15
challenges 9, 27, 44
communication 9, 16–17, 18–19, 34–35
  non-verbal 16, 17, 18, 33
  PECS 17
confidence 19, 22–23, 44
cyberbullying 35

dyslexia 10

exclusion 17, 33

family 9, 18, 26–27, 30, 31, 39, 45, 46
feelings 17, 33, 45
friends 9, 18, 27, 32, 33, 39

genes 15
getting help 6

inclusion 24–25, 28–29, 32–33, 36, 45, 46
interacting 8, 18–21
independence 11, 13, 30

learning difficulty 10, 40
  dyslexia 10
learning 8, 9, 12, 16, 23, 34, 36
learning disability diagnosis 6, 44
listening 18, 31, 33, 46

Makaton 16, 18
mobility 9, 11

online safety 34–35

personal care 9

respect 32, 40, 46

school 6, 9, 12, 17, 25, 27, 32–33, 35, 40
self-esteem 22, 44
stuttering 19

types of learning disability 8, 9, 13
  PMLD 9
  profound 8, 11